KNOWN AND NEW ANIMALS COLORING EDITION

Math Books for Kindergarten

Children's Math Books

BABY PROFESSOR

EDUCATION KIDS

Speedy Publishing LLC
40 E. Main St. #1156
Newark, DE 19711
www.speedypublishing.com
Copyright 2017

COUNT AND COLOR THE ANIMALS

ACTIVITY NO. 1

HOW MANY ANIMALS DO YOU SEE?

?

HOW MANY ANIMALS DO YOU SEE?

?

HOW MANY
MONKEYS
DO YOU SEE?

?

HOW MANY

BUNNIES

DO YOU SEE?

HOW
MANY
DOGS
DO YOU SEE?

HOW
MANY
CATS
DO YOU SEE?

?

ACTIVITY NO. 7

HOW MANY DOGS DO YOU SEE?

?

HOW MANY PIGS DO YOU SEE?

?

HOW MANY
BEARS
DO YOU SEE?

HOW MANY FISH DO YOU SEE?

HOW
MANY
COWS
DO YOU SEE?

?

HOW MANY

CHICKENS

DO YOU SEE?

ACTIVITY NO. 13

HOW MANY BIRDS DO YOU SEE?

?

HOW MANY HORSES DO YOU SEE?

?

HOW MANY GOATS DO YOU SEE?

?

HOW MANY

ELEPHANTS

DO YOU SEE?

HOW MANY ANIMALS DO YOU SEE?

HOW MANY INSECTS DO YOU SEE?

?

COUNT AND ADD THE ANIMALS.

1. + = (?)

2. + = (?)

3. + = (?)

1. + = (?)

2. + = (?)

3. + = (?)

1.  = (?)

2.  = (?)

3.  = (?)

1. + = (?)

2. + = (?)

3. + = (?)

1.  = ?

2.  = ?

3.  = ?

1.

2.

3.

1. + = (?)

2. + = (?)

3. + = (?)

1. + = (?)

2. + = (?)

3. + = (?)

COLOR BY NUMBERS

Coyote

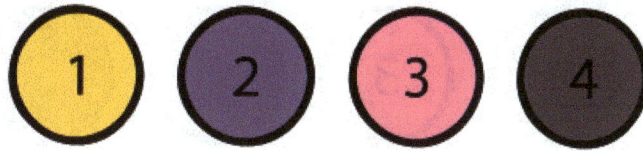

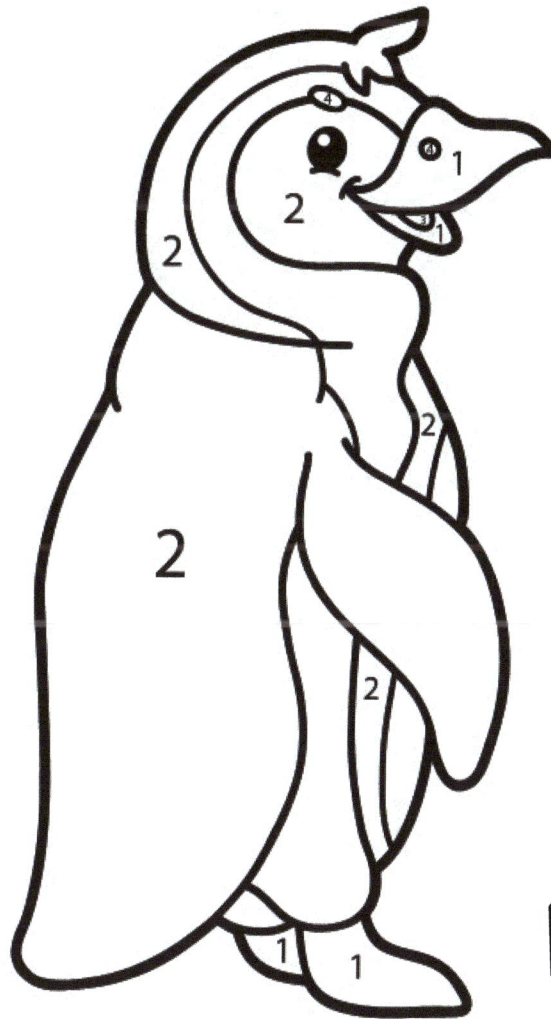

Penguin

Ram

Bull

Elephant

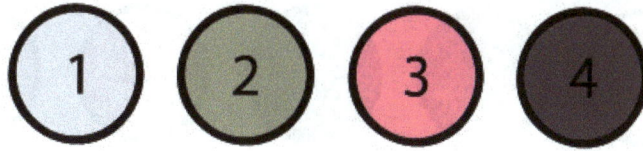

Rhinoceros

Koala

Horse

Lamb

Pig

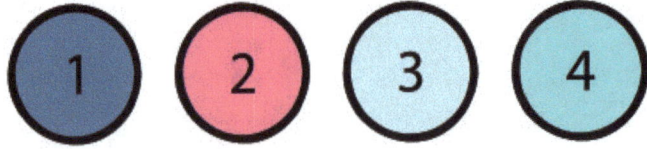

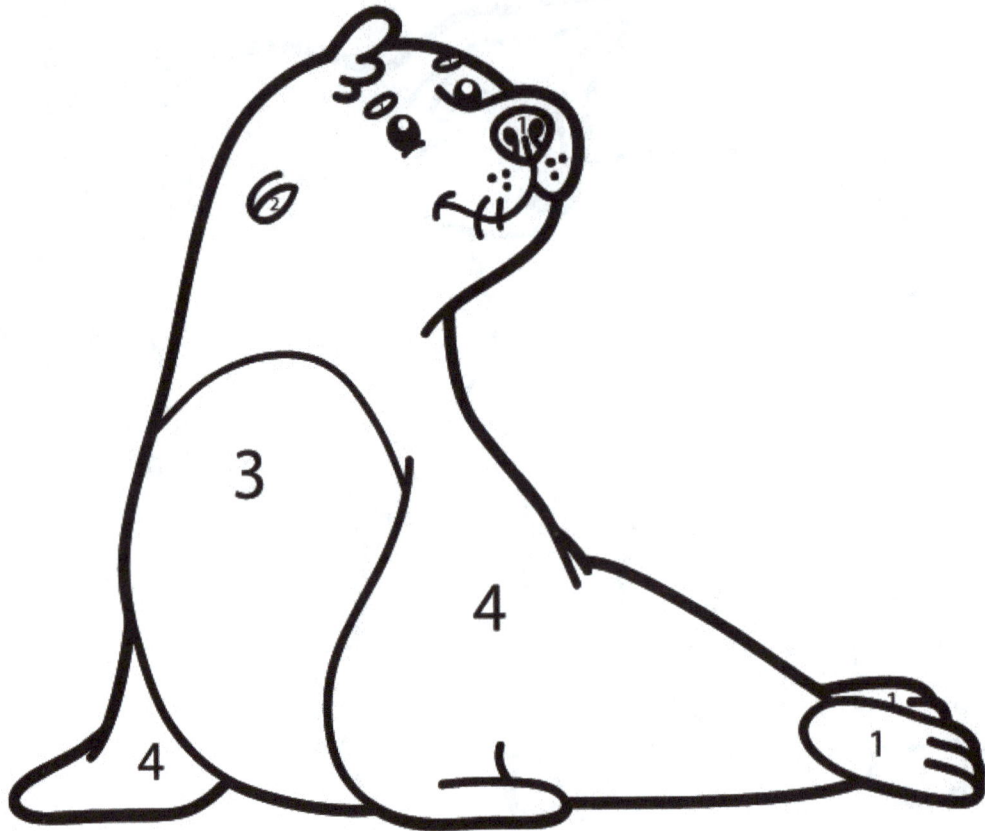

Seal

Hippopotamus

Lion

Frog

Bear

Whale

Toco Toucan
Bird

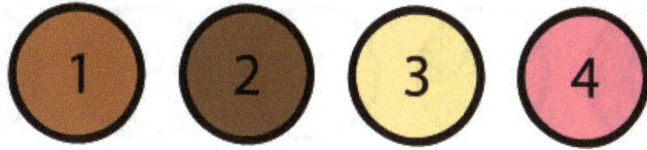

Dog

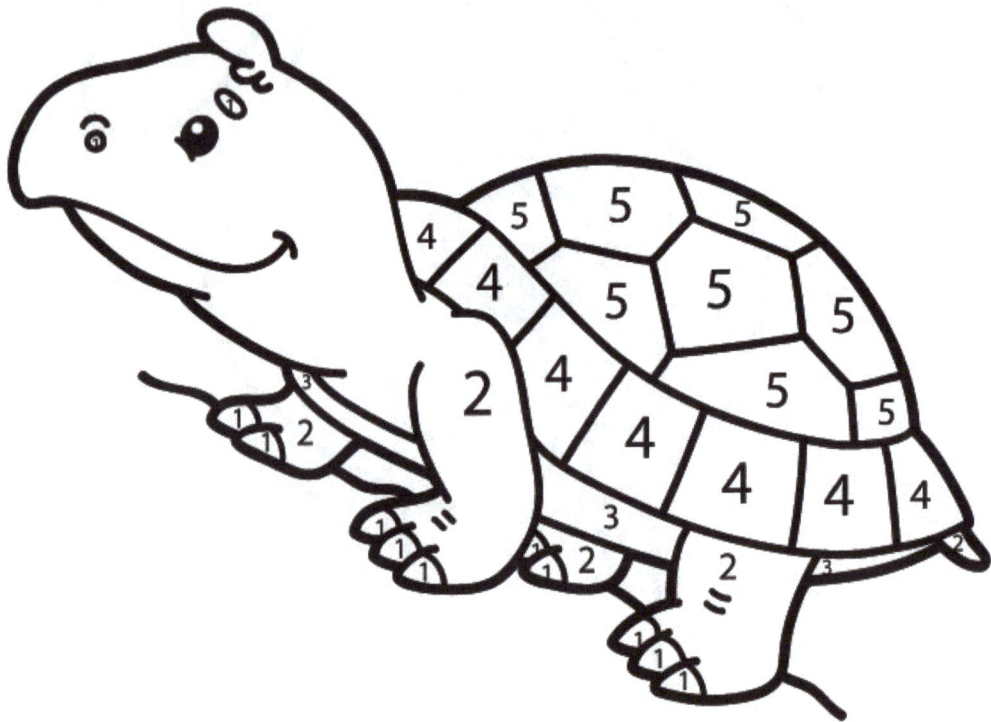

1 2 3 4 5

Turtle

Fish

Chicken

Zebra

ANSWERS!

ACTIVITY NO. 1

ANSWER
18

ACTIVITY NO. 2

ANSWER
15

ACTIVITY NO. 3

ANSWER
14

ACTIVITY NO. 4

ANSWER
21

ACTIVITY NO. 5

ANSWER
15

ACTIVITY NO. 6

ANSWER
16

ACTIVITY NO. 7

ANSWER
19

ACTIVITY NO. 8

ANSWER
13

ACTIVITY NO. 9

ANSWER
16

ACTIVITY NO. 10

ANSWER
12

ACTIVITY NO. 11

ANSWER
15

ACTIVITY NO. 12

ANSWER
13

ACTIVITY NO. 13

ANSWER
17

ACTIVITY NO. 14

ANSWER
14

ACTIVITY NO. 15

ANSWER
8

ACTIVITY NO. 16

ANSWER
10

ACTIVITY NO. 17

ANSWER
15

ACTIVITY NO. 18

ANSWER
19

1. + = 11

2. + = 14

3. + = 13

1. + = 10

2. + = 12

3. + = 9

1. + = 5

2. + = 8

3. + = 10

1. + = 2

2. + = 6

3. + = 9

1.  = 4

2.  = 9

3.  = 7

1.  = 13

2.  = 9

3.  = 6

ACTIVITY NO. 7

1.  + = 5

2.  + = 12

3.  + = 8

ACTIVITY NO. 8

1.  + = 9

2.  + = 19

3.  + = 8

Visit

BABY PROFESSOR
EDUCATION KIDS

www.BabyProfessorBooks.com

to download Free Baby Professor eBooks
and view our catalog of new and exciting
Children's Books

Milton Keynes UK
Ingram Content Group UK Ltd.
UKHW051132030924
447802UK00003B/175

9 798869 419026